CHANGE AND GROW

PUPPY TO DOG

Acknowledgements: Cover: getty images/Gary Randall, gettyimages/Dorling Kindersley, gettyimages/Dorling Kindersley, gettyimages/Martin Harvey. p1 gettyimages/Steve Shott, p2 gettyimages/Dorling Kindersley, p3 getty images/Photodisc, p5 gettyimages/Tracy Morgan, pp6–7 gettyimages/Jane Burton, p8 gettyimages/Time & Life Pictures, p9 gettyimages/ Dorling Kindersley, p10 gettyimages/Dorling Kindersley, p11 gettyimages/Dorling Kindersley, p12 gettyimages/Jane Burton, p13 gettyimages/Jane Burton, gettyimages/Tracy Morgan, p14 gettyimages/Steve Shott, p15 gettyimages/Steve Shott, p16 gettyimages/GK Hart/Vikki Hart, gettyimages/Martin Harvey, p17 gettyimages/Photodisc, p18 gettyimages/Tracy Morgan, gettyimages/Steve Lyne, p19 gettyimages/Stockbyte, p20 gettyimages/Gandee Vasan, p21 gettyimages/Dorling Kindersley, gettyimages/Steve Lyne, p22 gettyimages/GK Hart/Vikki Hart, p23 gettyimages/Dorling Kindersley, gettyimages/Gk Hart/vikki Hart, p24 gettyimages/Steve Shott.

First published by Parragon in 2009

Parragon
Queen Street House
4 Queen Street
Bath BA1 1HE, UK

Copyright © Parragon Books Ltd 2009

ISBN 978-1-4075-8045-6

Printed in China

CHANGE AND GROW

PUPPY TO DOG

LIVE. LEARN. DISCOVER.

Steve Parker

PaRragon

Bath · New York · Singapore · Hong Kong · Cologne · Delhi · Melbourne

A NEW LiFE BEGiNS

A newborn puppy is small and helpless. The day after it's born, you may think it is just a day old. But the puppy has already been growing inside its mother's body for nine weeks.

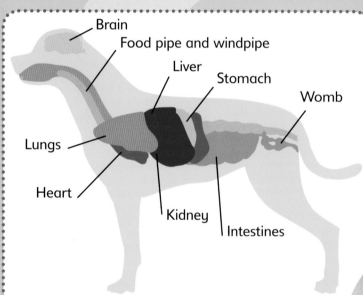

Brain
Food pipe and windpipe
Liver
Stomach
Womb
Lungs
Heart
Kidney
Intestines

Puppy's parents
The male and female dogs get together and mate. This makes the puppy start to grow.

Dad's coat is brown.

A safe place
The puppy grows inside a baglike part of the body called the womb. It gets food from its mother through a special tube called the cord.

Our puppies will be beautiful!

A puppy grows inside its mother for nine weeks—a baby elephant grows inside its mother for two years!

DiscoveryFact™

Look alike
Some of the puppies will look like Dad. Some will look like Mom. Some might look like a cross between the two.

Mom's ears are longer.

5

LiFE BEFORE BiRTH

When a female dog is carrying puppies, she is pregnant. She will probably have between four and six puppies growing and changing inside her.

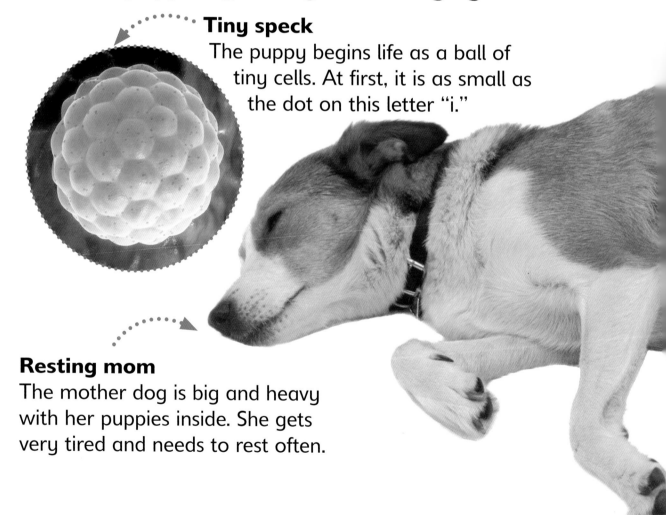

Tiny speck
The puppy begins life as a ball of tiny cells. At first, it is as small as the dot on this letter "i."

Resting mom
The mother dog is big and heavy with her puppies inside. She gets very tired and needs to rest often.

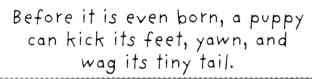

Taking shape

Safe inside its mother, the puppy's ears, eyes, nose, and mouth slowly develop. After a few weeks, it also has tiny paws and a very short tail.

Getting ready

Soon the puppy will start to grow some fur. It will be ready to enter the outside world in a few more weeks.

Ready to feed

The nipples on her belly swell with milk, ready to feed her puppies.

HERE I COME!

Puppies are usually born at night. The mother dog lies down quietly—and in the morning the puppies are there! She looks after each one carefully.

Somewhere safe

The mother chooses a safe, quiet place to have her puppies. She may get worried if there are other animals or people around.

Licked clean

The puppies are born one by one. The mother gently licks them clean and keeps them warm.

The new litter

It can take more than six hours for all the puppies to be born. The group of puppies is called a litter.

The largest recorded litter was 20 puppies—that's a lot of work for just one mother dog!

DiscoveryFact™

EAT, SLEEP, EAT, SLEEP

A new puppy is chubby and floppy, with short fur. Its eyes are shut, it cannot hear very well, and it has no teeth. But it has a good sense of smell!

First food
The puppies use their sense of smell to find milk. They wiggle up to a nipple, latch on, and take their first drink.

Each puppy has its own nipple.

Pushy pups
Sometimes the puppies push each other out of the way.

Newborn puppies need to eat every four to six hours through the day—and during the night, too!

DiscoveryFact™

Hungry pups
A good feeding can take half an hour. The puppies press their paws against their mother's belly to help the milk flow.

Sleepyheads
Newborn puppies snuggle up with their brothers and sisters to keep warm. When they are not eating, they sleep.

LEARNING FAST

A young puppy grows fast as it feeds on its mother's milk. After just one week, a puppy is twice as big as it was when it was born!

At first, the puppy cannot see well.

Eyes open
At two weeks, the puppy's eyes open. It can look around and see its family for the first time.

Wobbly walk

At three weeks old, the puppy can hear well. It tries to walk, but at first it wobbles a lot and falls over.

Food for thought

Then the puppy's teeth start to grow. It still drinks its mother's milk, but will also nibble solid puppy food from a bowl.

13

FUN AND GAMES

As the puppy grows bigger and stronger, it makes more noise and moves around more. By the time it is two months old, it no longer needs its mother's milk.

Play time

Every day, the puppy can run faster and jump higher. It plays games like "chase," "tug-of-war," and "play-fight" with its sisters and brothers.

Chew, chew

Puppies like to bite and chew things. This is how they learn about the world, and about what is good to eat and what is not.

A puppy has sharp teeth.

Leaving home

After two months, the puppy is ready to leave its mother, brothers, and sisters. It is time to start life with a new family.

Pet dogs are related to wild wolves, which were first tamed by people more than 12,000 years ago.

DiscoveryFact™

A NEW HOME

When a puppy first arrives at its new family home, it may whine and cry for its mother. It will settle down when it realizes its new home is a safe, happy place.

A place to sleep

The puppy needs a place of its own, where it can rest and sleep. A basket or box is perfect.

Play with me!

The puppy loves to play. It will chase toys and try to catch them. In the wild this would be good practice for hunting, but it is also great exercise.

That's my name
The puppy listens to its owners when they speak. If they say its name clearly and often, the puppy will soon learn what it is called.

The American coyote, the African wild dog, and the Australian dingo are three types of wild dog.

DiscoveryFact™

Hello, Max!

Good boy, Max!

GROWING UP FAST

By about four months old, the puppy is slimmer and stronger. It can run fast and jump high. It starts to get its grown-up teeth—and tests them by chewing even more!

Something to chew
The puppy chews for comfort when its new teeth are coming through. It needs its own toys to stop it from chewing things it shouldn't.

House training
At first, the puppy cannot control when it goes to the bathroom. It needs to learn to use an old newspaper. After a few months it should be "house-trained"—it can wait until it goes outside.

Adult dogs have 42 teeth—that's 10 more than a grown-up person, but 50 fewer than a dolphin!

DiscoveryFact™

Learning words

The puppy should slowly learn that it is part of a family—but not the boss. Its owners help it learn simple commands like "Sit!" "Stay!" and "Come!"

Come!

BEST BEHAVIOR

Young dogs need a lot of walks and exercise. They like to play with other dogs, but they need to learn not to get too excited so they don't bite or fight.

Collar and leash
The puppy needs to get used to wearing a collar and leash. It should be taught not to pull on the leash and to "heel."

Heel boy!
A dog that pulls hard on its leash can hurt its neck and have breathing problems.

A bark can be a warning.

A dog's sense of smell is 40 times better than a person's—they rely on their noses a lot more than we do!

DiscoveryFact™

Hush puppy

A young dog who gets into the habit of barking too much can become a problem. Its owners should teach it to stay quiet most of the time.

Being brushed

A dog keeps clean by licking its fur. Its owner should also groom it every day. This reminds the dog that it is part of a family, and that its owner is the boss!

ALL GROWN UP

By the time it is about one year old, the puppy is grown up and can have puppies of its own. Even though it has finished growing, it can still learn new things.

Help from the vet

Like people, dogs sometimes get sick or hurt. An animal doctor called a vet can help them get better.

Dog breeds

These are just a few of the many different breeds of dog.

There are over 400 breeds of dog— from tiny Chihuahuas to massive Great Danes.

DiscoveryFact™

Growing old

By about 10 years of age, some breeds of dogs are starting to get old. But others can live well past 20—and one reached 29!

Golden Retriever

Dalmatian

Bulldog

Alsatian

Westhighland Terrier

Spaniel

LiFE CYCLE

Mating
The male and female dogs mate. The puppy grows inside its mother for 9 weeks.

1 year
The puppy is now an adult dog. It can have puppies of its own.

Birth
The puppy is born and starts drinking its mother's milk.

32–40 weeks
The puppy is now almost full-grown.

1 to 2 weeks
The puppy's eyes open.

24–32 weeks
The puppy needs 2 meals a day, and lots of exercise and training.

2–3 weeks
The puppy's ears are now working properly.

16–24 weeks
The puppy chews a lot. Its muscles become much stronger.

3–6 weeks
The puppy's baby teeth grow. It starts to bark and wag its tail.

12–16 weeks
The puppy's adult teeth grow. It may try to become the family boss.

7–12 weeks
The puppy learns its name. It still needs 4 meals every day.

5–7 weeks
The puppy stops drinking its mother's milk and starts solid food.